DOWSING

This book explains the dowsing, or water-divining, phenomenon, its history and present-day application, and also how would-be dowsers can recognize and develop the ability. The author discusses the relative merits of the instruments available, and different aspects such as radiesthesia and map dowsing, as well as astral projection and its link with dowsing.

DOWSING
The Ancient Art of Rhabdomancy

by

ROBERT H. LEFTWICH

THE AQUARIAN PRESS
Wellingborough, Northamptonshire

First published 1976

© ROBERT H. LEFTWICH 1976

ISBN 0 85030 127 0 (UK)
ISBN 0 87728 313 3 (USA)

Filmset by Specialised Offset Services Ltd, Liverpool
Printed and bound in Great Britain by
Weatherby Woolnough, Wellingborough
Northamptonshire

CONTENTS

INTRODUCTION

Because the phenomenon of dowsing is an ability that manifests itself in such a personal manner, and because there seems to be little or no common ground upon which an indisputable explanation can be found for its existence, it is not going to be an easy matter to discuss the subject in acceptable terms and one is therefore inclined to report on one's own personal attitude and experience and hope it will be a guide to others possessing similar mental characteristics. However, that would not be fair and only of limited interest so I will include all known attitudes relevant to dowsing and its related activities.

Depending on our allocated characteristics, we tend to be governed by the attitude we adopt to the absorption of new knowledge and its interpretation. Those of a very rational make-up, frequently reject the idea of dowsing as being nonsensical, but there are those who are rather more analytically inclined and not only accept its existence but are prepared to devote much time to its useful development. Because my father was a mathematician and periodically had visitors of equal or greater thinking ability, I, as an only child, was frequently subjected to conversations quite beyond my understanding and although I was encouraged to listen, I invariably reverted to more pleasurable and lighter means of occupying myself. These discussions influenced me subconsciously, however, and later I became intensely interested in all matters appertaining to the mind and its uses, so I may well fit into that last category.

Subconscious Influence

At the other extreme, there are those rather emotionally unbalanced individuals who are very impressionable and, because of this instability, can easily be conditioned to think and feel any particular way regardless of their true thoughts. In reality, they are subconsciously influenced by suggestion to such a degree that when they witness or are informed that dowsing can be very tiring, they allow that thought to become instrumental in causing just such a realization when there is in fact no cause for it.

Many years ago, I attended a Congress of the British Society of Dowsers at the Spa Hotel in Tunbridge Wells during which a lecturer maintained he could 'neutralize' any subterranean stream, making it impossible for anyone to locate it. Not being prepared to accept such a bold statement, I openly challenged the speaker to do just that and, after allowing him sufficient time to locate and neutralize a suitable stream, most of us took the opportunity during the lunch break to seek the 'missing' stream in the hotel's car park. But, in spite of great enthusiasm, no one was able to find it and a number of competent dowsers were disappointed. In reality, they had all been mentally incapacitated through negative suggestion that it just was not there.

I personally could not accept such a situation. After all, had an experienced dowser not known about the 'neutralization', he would have had no difficulty in locating a stream that continues to exist and, accordingly, I had no difficulty in determining the stream's position, depth and flow – much to the concern of the lecturer and others.

First Attempts

I first realized I could dowse when, as a Sales Manager operating from home, I had occasion to drive through a particular country lane on three successive mornings. On the first one, workmen were digging a small trench at the side of the road, and when on the following day the original one had been filled and new operations begun on the opposite side, it occurred to me as a water engineer that they might conceivably have lost a main. On the third morning, when the centre of the road was being dug up, the position was irresistible and I stopped the car to make some enquiries. My guess was confirmed and, in addition, I was told that everything was all right now as their diviner had just arrived.

He duly walked over the area concerned with two L-shaped rods (in reality, bent welding rods) pointing outwards. On reaching the supposed water main, the rods slowly began to turn inwards. I was astounded, for I had heard of this activity but never witnessed it at such close range. Out of curiosity, I asked the gentleman if I could have a go and, to my utter amazement, I obtained an even greater response.

The originally planned working day immediately ceased to be of further interest and, on returning home and cancelling various appointments, I made up a pair of similar rods and began a series of experiments, both indoors and in the garden for I felt this ability had to be thoroughly investigated and developed. The next day I visited the County Library in Lewes where I discovered the existence of a British Society of Dowsers, the President of which was a Colonel A.H. Bell who lived in Cuckfield.

A meeting was later arranged, but in the meantime I could not resist writing a short article expressing my limited views on the subject for inclusion in a philosophical work I was preparing. I took it with me when I visited Colonel Bell to persuade him of my enthusiasm, and on reviewing it he published it in their journal before I had become a fully-fledged member. From that moment in time, my keenness and interest in the subject has increased constantly.

Increasing Knowledge

As recounted in Colin Wilson's book *Strange Powers*, I have always been intensely interested in all forms of ESP and the Occult. In an effort to increase this knowledge, I had built up quite a substantial library over the years, from which I was then able to extract much information on dowsing. This, backed by extensive experimentation, ultimately provided me with the required confidence I needed to face any application. This confidence began to manifest itself in the publication of more advanced articles in the BSD journal, which in turn were probably instrumental in my being appointed the Society's Official Dowser for Kent and Sussex.

Up to that time, most of my applications had arisen from personal recommendations, but on one occasion, whilst visiting friends in Mayfield, I mentioned this ability in passing and a very sceptical gentleman suggested it might be a good idea if I were to walk across his extensive lawns with a view to locating a buried twelve-inch drainage line. On stopping at the precise spot, he exclaimed with great enthusiasm that I was dead right and that we were now in business. The partnership didn't last very long as he was far too businesslike and in reality was only concerned with the potential profits, but through his contacts I was able to gain some useful experience. However, on becoming a Society's dowser, many other applications began to present themselves, some of which involved visiting distant lands.

A Natural Way of Life

In Nature, most forms of animal life, when confronted with loss of orientation or thirst, can usually sense the direction whereby any such deficiency can be corrected and no form of artificial instrumentation such as hazel twigs are necessary. On the other hand, we as human beings have become far too dependent on all kinds of artificial aids in our civilized way of life and in an effort to counteract this tendency, I have deliberately reverted to a more natural and ascetic way of life. Perhaps my adoption of certain principles would in reality be useless to many but because I had complete faith in my beliefs – the abstention from smoking, drinking and all harmful stimulants, combined with a rather monotonous vegetarian diet – they have been extremely effective in the development of both my dowsing and my other ESP faculties. In other words, the effect of adopting a very positive attitude of mind can be instrumental in the realization of one's desires.

Although the accepted term, dowsing, now incorporates a wide range of applications which include radiesthesia, radionics, horticulture and both the direct and indirect approaches to the location of subterranean matter and lost people, it is in reality part of our natural make-up which, over the past few centuries, has been permitted to deteriorate seriously due to lack of use and encouragement. But with a little perseverance, it can be reactivated in more people than is generally supposed. Being a natural process and part of the self-preservation principle, it is dormant in quite a number of us; in its more developed forms, a dowser requires no form of instrumentation. When it is present in women – who are usally subjected to far less of the artificialities and responsibilities of modern life, which discourage its development – it is invariably grouped under activities associated with 'intuition', but their forty per cent higher success rate is significant.

International Research
Since its more recent development at the beginning of this century, when Vicomte Henri de France published his famous work, *Le Sourcier Moderne*, a great deal of research has been carried out into the phenomenon of dowsing in many countries resulting in its general acceptance by quite a number of influential people in various fields of activity. Even whilst being very indirectly involved in the laying of a 500-mile, ten-foot water main near Los Angeles, I was informed by one of their senior employees that most of such companies in the United States utilized the services of a dowser to advise them on various problems likely to be encountered in their excavation work.

In Russia, too, the process is no longer considered to be in any way associated with the manifestations of wizardry or black magic, and many successful tests have been conducted in research programmes, resulting in its establishment in several useful fields of activity as 'The Biophysical Efforts Method'. In Japan, dowsing, among other uses, is commercially employed to determine the sex of pre-hatched eggs on conveyor belts, with the startling success rate of ninety-nine per cent.

Dowsing is therefore rapidly becoming a well and truly established phenomenon, although its real origin remains a mystery for most of us. Yet in Nature, there are countless signs of its indirect influence, such as the reluctance of animals, including pets, to sleep in certain areas which, on checking, invariably show that some subterranean water activity is present. There is, incidentally, evidence to support the claim that humans sleeping over existing streams encourage arthritic troubles. One of the more outstanding signs, however, is the accuracy with which elephants are able to locate underground water in times of drought, thereby indirectly serving humanity. Even gnats hovering in a column at a fixed height during a summer evening are in reality an indication of the existence of a concealed spring or small stream very near the surface, but their height above the ground unfortunately seems to bear no relationship to the water's depth.

Because of its very personal nature, what follows may well be highly controversial or even appear contradictory, but it is hoped that some of the contents of this book will assist both prospective dowsers and existing ones to see viewpoints other than their own.

CHAPTER ONE

THE HISTORY OF DOWSING

Because the so-called gift of dowsing is in reality one of our birthrights, it has always existed and consequently its origin is lost in antiquity. There have, however, been a number of outstanding dowsers who developed their potential powers to the point where they were able to contribute greatly to the comforts and benefits of mankind. To describe justifiably their activities in detail would necessitate biographical sketches quite beyond the scope of this book, and although their success rates were remarkably high, the methods and principles they employed for their realization varied greatly, suggesting that faith and sincerity of purpose were the underlying forces in common rather than the tapping and use of different sources of power.

All kinds of aids to dowsing have been devised by man in an effort to widen his range of sensitivity and many influential individuals have concluded from personal experimentation that certain methods of approach were more rewarding than others. This is to be expected, of course, but in recording and passing on this acquired information to others, many recipients have unknowingly been preconditioned to react in a very similar manner, when in reality quite a different self-imposed approach might well have proved to be far more productive.

A More Realistic Approach

I am not suggesting that we should all operate in precisely the same way, for individuality must be recognized, but when it is realized that so many competent dowsers of today continue to be influenced by the dictates of the past, it is time a more realistic approach was adopted to encourage a greater degree of conformity.

Apart from the many instruments man has devised to increase the sensitivity of his dowsing faculty, there also exist countless attitudes of mind, making the whole process one of a very personal nature. Yet I cannot but feel that, as with any 'art', there should be a most practical and efficient way of obtaining results. Perhaps art is the wrong word as it immediately conjures up limitless variations of personal preference, which is the very thing to be avoided. We are all human and although we possess different abilities capable of varying development, the sincere application of self-analysis combined with an open attitude of mind on planned experimentation should show some evidence of a uniform pattern.

In most other forms of human activity, it has not been too difficult to determine the best and most efficient way of obtaining results, but with dowsing no particular method of approach has ever been found to be generally acceptable. It is obvious we still cannot expect to understand fully the underlying forces involved in dowsing, for the problem has been with us for thousands of years, but it should not have been an insurmountable problem to ascertain whether the applied forces originated from the mind, the body or extraneous sources.

Mental Process

To satisfy oneself that the process is one of mental origin rather than one brought about through bodily reactions is simplicity itself. Where a narrow buried object such as a pipeline is known to exist, walk towards it in a fully upright position and it will be found that the rods or pendulum will react when one's body or heels are vertically above the pipes. Now repeat the action bending the body forwards and it will be found that the rods will be motivated immediately one's head is vertically above the pipe.

Physical reactions certainly take place and the instruments used are merely means of amplifying mentally activated movements which have probably weakened through both lack of use and the detrimental influences of Society's artificial conditioning process, so it is just possible that in our very distant past these movements might have been instrumental in instinctively guiding man to satisfy his needs. Anyway, with a little perseverance most potential sensitives possessing the ability can greatly encourage its further development. If our mental reactions were in some inexplicable way activated by Nature's external physical forces, many hypersensitive individuals would be permanently subjected to an undesirable awareness bordering on discomfort. This just is not the case for the existence of personal control indicates that, in all probability, the process is a self-contained one within ourselves.

Ancient Superstitions

Superstition and the adoption of erroneous ideas have also greatly influenced the art and this is fully substantiated by the contents of old manuscripts and publications on the subject. It was at one time (and perhaps still is by some) believed that the rod itself attracted objects to varying degrees, so special lists were prepared from experience which indicated that gold, copper, iron, silver, tin, lead, coal, limestone and water produced signal strengths in just that descending order of value. Whenever practicable, therefore, rods were made from similar material to assist in the 'attracting' process, but this did not explain the equal successes obtained by those not equipped with the more expensive units. In a way, the generally accepted idea of using samples may well have originated from this particular approach.

However, contrary to the sample theory, another ancient school of thought maintained that to locate a particular metal, it was necessary to prepare a powdered mixture of all other known metals *not* required and to have this injected into a specially hollowed-out section of a baguette. The concoction would then be sealed in, thereby ensuring that its user would only respond to what had been *omitted*. Because this was believed, it worked for many – even to the extent of causing a sample to repel a baguette being held by a dowser *intending* to locate that particular material. This suggests that any professional dowser of that period needed to possess no end of 'tools' to justify likely applications.

It was also believed that the basic twig had to have its particular specification and originate from the right kind of tree – not one capable of bearing fruit or nuts as these would seriously hinder the selective process, with the exception of water. So one is once more faced with contradictions. The position of our planets and other astral bodies were also believed to play their part in the dowsing faculty, but if one were to believe in all the supposed potential influences likely to affect the process, it would not have survived to the present day. It is, as has been emphasized, quite a simple process.

The Two Categories

In principle, dowsers can be classified into two main categories. There are the more natural folk attached to the simpler ways of life, such as those associated with farming communities. This is particularly applicable to the West Country where, in the fifteenth century, German dowsers came over here to assist us in the location of lost tin mines. But, in being aware of their gift, this group don't seem to be concerned with its development, so their abilities are frequently restricted to the location of water and not its depth, direction of flow or yield.

The other category seems to consist of individuals belonging to the more sophisticated side of our society who, on being enlightened of its existence, realize they possess a latent interest in the subject which, under the influence of Society's conditioning process, becomes more analytically inclined. This, combined with the realization of a dormant ability, can in certain cases lead to the development of a high degree of sensitivity and consequential success in that field.

Although the art and its infinite variations have reached a high level of reliability, there is no doubt that, with the readjustment of our personal views on life, higher levels of achievement and success can be realized. But they may well necessitate a lowering of our so-called artificial standards and values, and to the majority such an idea is totally unacceptable.

All dowsing is in effect merely a means whereby some of our natural instincts and abilities can be confirmed in a practical and satisfying manner, for the required knowledge is within most of us anyway. If the right mental attitude is developed, or at least encouraged, in the first place, the answers to problems other than those solved through dowsing would be ours for the asking, for it is the extension of this mental principle, if taken to its logical conclusion, that produces those few enlightened individuals from whom we can learn so much.

Recorded Information

Many references could be made to dowsers of the distant past but their achievements were not backed by accompanying explanations of their ability, because the art was invariably shrouded in secrecy. The first documentary record of dowsing was made in 1518 when Martin Luther condemned the practice as being the work of the Devil or Black Magic, which was strange since his father was a miner and consequently he must have seen the rods in operation on many occasions.

On the other hand, there is a wealth of recorded information available on the various theories of dowsing put forward by practitioners over the last century, and several books on the subject are available.

Of the countless examples that could be given to demonstrate the unlikelihood of certain theories put forward to account for particular reactions, reference is made to the distinguished French dowser, Vicomte Henri de France, who amongst others maintained that the discovery of electricity was an incalculable aid to all those having a desire to develop the dowsing faculty, for both the rods and the pendulum could easily be activated through simple experiments on electric currents and magnetic fields.

Also, and because of its added advantage of

variable length regulation, he believed the pendulum had far greater potential even to the degree of being able to be tuned in to what presumably were harmonic multiples of high-frequency signals emitted from radio stations, but when, in the light of modern knowledge, we appreciate the degree of accuracy that would be needed to adjust the supporting thread to just such a frequency response (and of course maintain it beyond a fraction of time to make it recognizable whilst being held by the hand), the whole idea becomes ludicrous.

I am not suggesting that he did not succeed in his abilities but the explanations he offered to account for his remarkable achievements were not directly attributable to the reception of electro-magnetic waves. It is true that, basically, we function and are motivated through the transmission of minute electrical signals originating from the brain which can be measured with powerful amplifiers called Electroencephalographs, but on being subjected to this machine whilst undergoing various tests at St Batholomew's Hospital during the preparation of a television programme where I was to dowse under controlled conditions, no response or indication of unusual activity could be detected so it was concluded that quite another form of 'communication' was taking place.

Unreliable 'Facts'

Many of the suggestions made, even by experienced dowsers, can have far-reaching effects and on many occasions when I have used metal rods in the process of locating lost objects made from the same metal in the presence of other dowsers, they have commented that I was wasting my time and would never succeed as 'the two metals were neutralizing each other', so my inexplicable success was attributed to luck. There are so many who have knowingly been conditioned into believing certain 'facts' from the unreliable experience of others that much doubt now exists as to the authenticity of dowsing.

Three British Dowsers

In more recent years, there have of course been many successful and well-known dowsers who have indirectly influenced others with their ideas and reactions, and although countless references could be made to so many who have lived in France and other parts of Europe, particular mention should be made of three British dowsers.

W.S. Lawrence who lived from 1810 to 1896 and spent most of his life in Bishopston, Bristol, was very active in this field for almost seventy years, whilst being both a stonemason and holding various parochial appointments. He was one of those dowsers who, on applying his ability, would suffer greatly from muscular spasms resulting in extreme exhaustion when the selected work was of prolonged duration. For the general location of minerals and water, he invariably used a flat steel wire bent into the shape of a horse shoe, but for the particular detection of water, it was necessary for him to use a robust forked hazel twig, thereby indicating that in some way he had unknowingly conditioned his own mental attitude to a particular approach which, when witnessed by easily influenced outsiders also having the desire to encourage their abilities in that direction, would have its effect.

As a water engineer, there were a number of occasions when I visited Messrs John Mullins and Sons Ltd, whose offices are adjacent to Sevenoaks station. It wasn't until my second appointment that I realized the company was in fact the one formed by John Mullins in Colerne, Wiltshire, in 1882. John Mullins was a mason working with his father and was on the site of a house being constructed by Sir John Ould on the Ashwick Estate in Gloucestershire in 1859, when a professional dowser visited it. When Mullins was tested later, an instant response was experienced. But it wasn't until 1882 that he decided to give up his work as a mason and devote his time and energies to dowsing.

His attitude to payment resembled mine in many ways for he would only charge a fee if results were forthcoming and when operations were restricted to a local area. This is a practical and commendable proposition but in this modern age, where time is money and travelling expenses have to be accounted for, a more materialistic approach is necessary, and when his two sons took the business over, many changes were made.

One of John Mullins' firm beliefs was that dowsing should preferably be carried out with a newly picked forked twig to ensure pliability and maximum sensitivity; on reaching one's quest, the fork would turn upwards with a violence of action proportional to both the volume and proximity of the water being located.

S.T. Child was a miller's son who became fascinated by dowsing when he saw one of the wells being cleaned out at his father's works in the village of Croscombe, Somerset, where water was scarce, in the presence of a dowser using a watch spring. On trying out the same process later, he discovered he was the only one in the family endowed with this natural gift.

He tried a number of experiments and in due course was challenged to locate water in an area not likely to be very productive. He was so successful that the yield from the combination of the three closely positioned springs he located turned out to be sufficient to meet the needs of the entire village at that time.

Some years later he moved his business to near Hadleigh, East Anglia, and although he tried to practise water-finding more as a recreation from the routine of everyday work, the success which attended his efforts became so widely known through the Press and hearsay that this activity became a business in itself, resulting in his becoming extremely well known in East Anglia at the end of the last century. He wrote a small book entitled *Water Finding* which was published by the *East Anglian Daily Times* in 1902.

Dowsing in France

France has always been active in the dowsing field and the famous seventeenth-century minerologists, Baron and Baroness de Beausoleil, were largely responsible for establishing the art on a more acceptable basis, at the same time attempting to establish France as a leading European power through its mineral wealth. Though their efforts were rather short-lived due to their involvement in the conspiracy of St Mars, they did have a great deal of success and this was reflected in various published works. The most famous of these was *La Physique Occulte ou Traite de la Baguette Divinatoire* by the Abbé of Vallemont, in which he expounded his theories on the use of samples and fields, many of which are retained by dowsers to this day.

Many other French dowsers have been active in their respective ways but one of the more outstanding contributors to the field was Michel Eugene Chevreul. His book, *De la Baguette Divinatoire*, written in 1854, became the accepted treatise on the subject for quite a long time and was indirectly responsible for the publication of other works in this field.

Different Viewpoints

Since that time, there have been dowsers from all walks of life who have expressed their viewpoint as to the fundamental cause for the phenomenon, but in reality it is doubtful if anyone will ever be able to explain and interpret the forces involved fully. The authors of *The Divining Rod*, Sir William Barrett and Theodore Besterman, were of the opinion that a dowser was a person endowed with a subconscious supernormal cognitive faculty, unknown to him but absorbed into the subconscious and revealed by means of an unconscious muscular reaction – or, less often, by an obscure nervous sensation or emotion which produces physiological disturbances – or, very rarely, by means of direct supernormal cognition made conscious by a visualization or hallucination.

In bygone days (and, to a limited extent, today), it was often thought by outsiders that the dowsing faculty was in some way related to witchcraft. If, by this, they inadvertently meant the use or misuse of mind which could be instrumental in the materialization or destruction of our subconscious desires, I would definitely agree.

The basic characteristics of humanity have not been changed by history and, because modern dowsers are completely unaware of the forces they are tapping, they do not realize the potential power at their disposal. Although invariably utilized to benefit humanity through healing and other useful means, this can just as easily be channelled along different lines to provide almost unlimited scope in many other fields, including anti-social activity. When these forces are combined with the ability to consciously create circumstances, almost all desires can be realized.

CHAPTER TWO

THE RADIATION THEORY

In an effort to determine what forces were at work in the dowsing process, one of the first experiments I tried was the application of various attitudes of mind whilst walking over both known and unknown buried objects, and it was soon found that by concentrating on a particular object all other items were automatically eliminated. These findings were largely opposed to the teachings I gained both from my own books and those given to me by experienced practitioners, for in my earlier days it was quite strongly impressed upon me that to be selective in locating anything, it was necessary to 'tune in' to the object being sought by holding in one's hand a sample of it so that its radiations could be more keenly felt and accurately interpreted. I soon realized that such an approach was only needed when the mind was unfamiliar with the object being sought, and that once the required information was known it was quite unnecessary to continue making physical contact with a sample unless one's concentrational powers were exceptionally limited.

In support of this claim, I came across an old dowser in Spain who firmly believed in the sample school of thought and when I persuaded him to try a different but more positive approach, he was astounded to find that after a few attempts it worked. He immediately disposed of a large collection of samples which, up to that time, he was convinced were indispensable to his 'trade'.

Again, I had occasion some years ago to visit the County Administration Offices in Crawley on business and happened to see the 'Revealer' on the desk of a surveyor. This is a very expensive dowsing instrument consisting in principle of two L-shaped, well balanced rods fitting loosely in supporting bearings, on the front of which is a network of wires holding selective phials containing various appropriate samples for the hand. Being interested, I naturally enquired into its use and was informed that only one of their staff could use it to advantage, and that the samples were a quite useless refinement as far as their operator was concerned.

No doubt, I shall find myself being severely criticized both by members of the BSD and by others who do not agree with my findings, but having conducted extensive experiments in all aspects of the dowsing phenomenon, I am certain that the active forces involved originate from the mind which is in itself a wonderful computer that can be programmed to most of our desires. It is because of its ability to be programmed that so many good dowsers unknowingly allow themselves to be falsely conditioned into getting their results very indirectly through the use of various aids believed to be necessary. Unfortunately, once they are set in their ways and consistently obtain satisfactory results using a particular method, few are going to be persuaded to try a different approach. Yet, if one were to be a little more objective and analytically inclined, such a change might well prove to be thoroughly worth while.

The Influence of Colour

There are those who firmly believe that there exists an important relationship of colour to matter, and that these radiations can greatly influence their results. In accepting this approach, the mind will adjust itself to the indirectness of the procedure and ultimately produce the same results, but such a process is unnecessarily complicated. But it was for this method that Mager's Rosette, which is a flat disc sub-divided into eight coloured segments, came into existence. By placing a finger on a pre-selected colour, the mind of the operator is unknowingly preconditioned to eliminate all other possibilities being sought because, subconsciously, the relationship between each colour and its representation has been well and truly predetermined, and consequently no difficulty is experienced in locating the lost object.

This is such an amazing idea that I couldn't resist trying another experiment. I blindfolded myself and walked over a known stream (being aware that the accepted colour for water was cobalt violet) but my reactions were in no way influenced by the position of my finger on the disc. I am not denying that colour can play an important role and greatly influence our lives but its use and introduction to the dowsing field is grossly overrated, and, on further analysis, probably quite unnecessary.

The Questioning Process

Since it is generally accepted that the mind controls the body, it is obvious that it must be connected with the dowsing process in some way, regardless of the other explanations put forward, and this is fully substantiated by the procedure followed by most competent dowsers who pose themselves 'questions' when isolating various possibilities in their selection process. Anyone possessing a reasonable degree of sensitivity can try dowsing over a known subterranean stream, and deliberately ask themselves 'Is coal present here?' or 'Does a cavity exist here?', only to observe the rods remaining motionless; on asking for the presence of water, however, instant reactive movements follow.

Insulating Materials

Many dowsers genuinely believe they cannot function when wearing gym shoes or wellington boots or are in any way subjected to conditions involving the presence of insulating materials likely to restrict or obstruct the emission of 'Earth's natural conductive radiations', and yet many successful tests have been carried out and have proved conclusively that any such restrictions are self imposed through auto-suggestion.

Many years ago, I had occasion to meet an experienced dowser from the BSD and, having persuaded him to co-operate with me on an experiment in the interests of the dowsing fraternity, I invited him to dowse for the stream feeding my garden well. When he had located it without any difficulty, I positioned some wide boarding over the relevant area, explaining to him that I had made up two grey-coloured sheets – one of a non-conductive plastic and the other of galvanized iron – and that it was my intention to substitute one for the other without his knowledge, to ascertain its effect on his reactions. In reality, only the plastic sheet existed, and this remained in position throughout. When I informed him of the presence of the supposed metal one, he experienced no difficulty in re-locating the stream, but on being told the plastic sheet had been substituted, his rods remained motionless.

Knowing his beliefs in that direction, I never told him the true position as such a disclosure would have been very unkind and might well have undermined his confidence, but it proved conclusively to me that the process was very closely related to mental attitude and that an extremely positive outlook was essential at all times if a really high degree of reliability was to be attained.

The Radiation Theory
Many explanations have naturally been put forward to account for the dowsing faculty. In principle, they fall into two main categories, neither of which in my view adequately explains certain extensions of the phenomenon. The first one, which for lack of a recognized name, I have called the Radiation Theory, is that all matter emits some kind of radiation and, depending on the sensitivity of the operator, he is subconsciously able to sense and differentiate one radiation from another.

Such a theory may appear to be superficially plausible and no doubt satisfied many less demanding dowsers of the past when most operations were limited to the location of actual matter, but today it does not in any way explain the location of voids such as are frequently encountered in archaeological surveys associated with new construction work. Two years ago I was approached by an American oil company who, during the construction of a large refinery in Spain, had come across a vast network of subterranean irrigation tunnels belonging to a bygone age, some of which reached a depth of fifty feet. Numerous efforts had been made to locate them with the help of mechanized equipment but even when one was located, its course could never be determined. Before my arrival, it appeared that they had decided to resort to gigantic excavations with bulldozers but this approach didn't prove to be very effective either, and in any case was far more costly than my services.

The absence of radiations is significant, and the fact that they have no hindering effect on a dowser seeking cavities can be explained, but to be asked to believe in the radiation theory, which also supports the claim that a dowser can supposedly isolate a particular radiation emanating from a lost object thousands of miles away (in what must from his point of view be an environment bombarded with radiations from all directions), is too unrealistic to say the least and there must obviously be other reasons or forces at work to account for such remarkable accomplishments.

The Radar Principle

Originally, I was asked to devote an entirely separate section to the second recognized method of approach but as it is so closely allied to the radiation or telluric emission theory, I felt it should be incorporated under the same heading.

I have called it the Radar Principle because, though man has made much so-called progress with his advanced scientific discoveries through the ages, in reality there is little he can invent that doesn't already exist in Nature in one form or other.

In principle, it is thought that, like bats, we possess a built-in system capable of emitting some form of high-frequency signal which, on its reflection from an article being sought, can be re-interpreted to provide desired information. Unlike bats, however, we possess no directional control, so if such an idea is adopted, the resulting signals would be emitted in all directions from the brain, resulting in extreme waste and the production of only a few useful radiations for any particular application. When it is realized that reliable information can be received from great distances, it is difficult to believe in such an explanation, although their penetration to shallow depths in surface dowsing seems just feasible until we appreicate that it would be vital to remain perfectly still whilst working, and this of course does not happen.

Indirect Dowsing

Neither of these explanations can account for the more remote processes of medical radiesthesia and particularly indirect dowsing where a competent dowser can tap the mind of any individual from a distance to provide required information.

When I mentioned this last application during the preparation of the television programme 'Margins of the Mind', Brian Inglis expressed scepticism and in an effort to convince him of the reality of such an ability, I allowed myself to be blindfolded whilst a non-dowser belonging to the production staff was asked to walk towards an area where a drain was known to exist. I experienced no difficulty in locating it, but, though from my point of view the demonstration was very relevant to the dowsing process, it was considered to be off the record and therefore was not included in the programme as it was thought too many viewers might have interpreted it as being associated with the controversial practices of witchcraft and magic.

Looking at the whole position from a very detached viewpoint, it would appear that, regardless of the different attitudes adopted, both groups are capable of producing astounding results. In my view, this suggests that a greater overriding power is in fact being tapped and this is largely indifferent to superficial personal attitudes provided it is respected and not excessively abused. With regard to this last point, I have met many dowsers who had charged excessive fees for their services over a prolonged period and on awakening one morning suddenly found that their gift had disappeared. Now, whether these occurrences were due to the manifestation of a self-imposed guilt complex or the intervention of forces beyond our understanding, no one can say, but it is a reminder that some of the good things in life should be handled with care.

CHAPTER THREE

PROJECTION OF THE SUPERCONSCIOUS, AND ASTRAL PROJECTION

A far more satisfying explanation than those described in the last chapter is needed and I feel that the partial projection of the superconscious is better able to account for the different levels of development in this field than any other theory so far put forward. We all understand the terms conscious and subconscious but are possibly less familiar with the superconscious which represents a part of our minds capable of being detached and projected from the body to anywhere we please. It is in reality a form of conscious astral travel, as opposed to its unconscious counterpart where the body's basic functions are controlled by the subconscious and the rest of the mind has unlimited spatial freedom.

Although the mechanics of such a theory are not easy for the Westerner to understand, it does provide an explanation for both surface dowsing and its more remote versions such as map dowsing or radionics. The energies being tapped probably belong to powers that can in principle be used either for the betterment of mankind or for its potential destruction, as they are closely allied to those practised in witchcraft. Careless experimentation can therefore be dangerous. In fact, religious organizations wished to employ my services on two separate occasions, one of which entailed the location of Dead Sea Scrolls, but on hearing I was a dowser the directors turned me down on the grounds that they wished to have no dealings with the works of the Devil.

An Etheric Counterpart

I have attempted to clarify the related process of conscious astral travel and astral projection but to describe in detail the various complex processes involved in the relationship would be an impossibility, as it is purely an individualistic experience varying with different people and controlled by little known forces. The fundamental concept, however, is that man possesses an etheric counterpart which under normal conscious conditions coincides with his physical body but, depending on his natural periodicity or bio-rhythm, this can be partially or completely projected from it.

In this condition, he is frequently able to see himself as a separate entity and, after some experience, can project his ethereal body, or 'vehicle of the soul' as it is sometimes termed, quite a distance from the physical body, although he is usually very much aware of the existence of an ethereal connection between the two.

The Silver Cord

This connection usually manifests itself as a 'silver cord' which can normally be seen to leave the forehead of the physical body and enter the etheric counterpart at the back of the neck.

It is said by those in authority that, provided this connection remains visible and intact, there is no danger and normal life can be resumed at will, but should it be severed or damaged in any way, the immediate disintegration of the physical body would begin. How anyone can make such a startling remark is quite beyond me but I do believe there are countless variations in this extremely personal process. I for one have left my body on many occasions and have never to date seen this so called 'silver cord' or anything resembling it. Only a few years ago, I was experimenting with these powers and, having left my body, I suddenly became aware that I had entered the bedroom of a dowser friend of mine living in Southern Ireland, who happened to be a member of the BSD. I realized from his reactions that he had seen me and two days later, I received a letter from him confirming my 'visit'.

In many ways, this temporary detachment from consciousness resembles biological hibernation. The normal functioning rates for most of the body's activities fall to a level just above that necessary to sustain life, and on returning to normal consciousness, a certain degree of over-compensation can at times take place, resulting in a temporary slight rise in body temperature and heart rate.

The Purpose of Astral Projection

In our present stage of mental development, we are obliged to conclude that there must be a purpose for the existence of astral projection, but apart from being a possible indication of man's potential ability to reach higher planes of enlightenment, the reasons are by no means obvious. It may make its appearance for the acquirement of specialized knowledge such as the various fields of activity discussed in this book, and if so it appears to be restricted to those best able to benefit from its use, which may well be intentional on the part of the unknown forces permitting its existence. I say 'restricted' because the egotistical, greedy individuals possessing such a gift would no doubt try to exploit it by 'willing' themselves to be in places necessitating secrecy in the interests of maintaining social order. On the other hand, perhaps such a gift rarely makes itself known to the kind of person likely to abuse it although it can be brought about through artificial means such as drug-induced comas or possibly the use of anaesthetics. Fortunately, the idea of astral-travel or dowsing for material gain under such conditions is impractical.

A further explanation offered assumes that all humanity is physically imperfect and that the faults remain undetected during immaturity but become more apparent in later life. These have a varying amount of influence on our ability to maintain the tight bond that holds our ethereal and physical bodies together without which full control is not always possible.

Just as it is extremely difficult to describe the detaching process in astral projection with any clarity, so the achieved condition for space and time is different from our normal conception of these values. They are so changed, indeed, that they become virtually non-existent, as is sometimes experienced by thinkers excessively absorbed in abstract thought in their private world devoid of physical matter.

Drawback of an Analytical Approach

Because of the difficulty in being able to demonstrate or prove the existence of this subtle etheric body, orthodox science has largely discredited the whole idea as unrealistic. This may be because scientists have conditioned themselves to being too materialistic in their analytical approach, thereby greatly discouraging the possible development of any such latent power within themselves.

Complete proof for those not able to experience these unusual powers is not really possible, other than by observing the results obtained from their use in the various fields of activity under discussion.

Several explanations can be found to justify or account for any peculiar ability, but the very fact that many normal and perfectly well-balanced dowsers can experience these detached physical states in varying degrees greatly supports if not confirms their existence. Some are occasionally aware of an inner sensation of 'lightness' but, due to lack of knowledge, attribute their feelings to overwork when in reality a condition conducive to projection is making itself known.

First Projection in Childhood

In fact, many sensitive individuals experience their first involuntary projection during childhood on being put to bed but, because of the fear of being misunderstood and thought to possess some mental abnormality, many children retain this knowledge from their parents, thereby creating the very mental conditions they are trying to avoid. Such powers sometimes become apparent in hyper-sensitive people on retirement to a more natural way of life than they led during their working days.

In the earlier stages of our development, they may occur either voluntarily or involuntarily, but in nearly all cases the detachment from reality will have taken place through no obvious external cause. After some prolonged experimentation, these projections can be produced at will within one's periodicity cycle and can frequently be controlled and directed as required.

Once this higher degree of mental control is

attained, little doubt is left as to the partial destiny of man's soul. Death need no longer be feared for it is merely a painless transformation from our existing state to a supposedly superior one. Once experienced, the whole of one's attitude towards the more conventional Western approaches to life and religion become completely revolutionized and all past fears of the future are dispersed.

Developing the Ability

It is true that we are all made differently and what suits one personality need not necessarily suit another, but anyone developing or having just discovered his ability to dowse – and it is believed that twenty-five per cent of the population are potential dowsers – should keep an open mind on the subject and be very selective in his absorption of the wide range of information available. If, however, he is strong willed and exceptionally analytically inclined, he can afford to listen to every viewpoint and combine this knowledge with useful personal experimentation. This can then lead to the development of self-confidence and reliability, making the demand for the services of such an individual very great. But anyone who does not possess these characteristics and is susceptible to suggestion may well find himself in a state of mental confusion.

For example, one can deliberately programme one's mind to react differently from the normally accepted pattern of events by imposing an overriding order to the 'computer' brain. This causes the rods or whatever means are employed to remain active everywhere *except* where the selected object is to be located, and then and *only* then will the rods remain motionless. Such

experiments should be restricted to those with
extensive experience in this field who have no
doubts as to their abilities.

Suggestion can also be instrumental in
activating the faculty. On many occasions I have
met interested parties wishing to try dowsing
who, when subjected to a number of tests with
different instruments over an existing tunnel,
stream or pipe line in my garden, would feel
nothing; but when their true positions were
disclosed to them, a proportion of them would
instantly sense a reaction and in no time be able
to locate objects on their own. This indicates that
in all probability far more than twenty-five per
cent possess the ability although, needless to
add, they would be unable to differentiate one
object from another.

Cumulative Effects of Suggestion

Although suggestion activated by the association
of ideas obtained through experience can be
highly beneficial, it can also be devastatingly
destructive due to its cumulativeness, so it is
imperative that a detached, overriding, rational
approach or control be developed, which can be
tapped to restore our equilibrium should things
suddenly begin to go inexplicably wrong.

Not long ago, before setting off for a coastal
tour on personal business, a number of things
began to go wrong. When I was preparing my
picnic, I broke the top of my Thermos flask. I
then burned a patch on the inside of my
sheepskin coat in an effort to dry it on top of the
stove. When I was about to leave, the car began
to make strange noises which I later discovered
were caused by a broken circulating water
pump, and when I did at last get moving, one of
my tooth fillings dropped out. That was the

limit. I stopped the car and, with the application of severe concentration, readjusted my attitude which in some way had been influenced by negative forces (or from self-imposed ones) and there were no more undesirable incidents – in fact, the very reverse was the case and I had a successful day.

This particular story has little bearing on our subject but it does provide a typical example of the potential power all of us have at our disposal to readjust our attitudes to a more positive approach, and when this is applied to the process of dowsing, it can greatly increase the success rate.

A brief reference has already been made to the fact that some people are capable of experiencing physical exhaustion as a result of a prolonged dowsing session, whilst others assert that they suffer from sensations ranging from peculiar tingling reactions in the limbs to decidedly unpleasant pains in the epigastric regions. But why should this be? If it really is a process entirely activated by the mind, which is perpetually active, why should I be able to dowse throughout several consecutive days in a semi-tropical climate and not feel the slightest ill effects whilst equally experienced dowsers operating under winter conditions in England become thoroughly worn out after only a short session, thereby necessitating several hours of rest to recuperate? The cause must be of psychological origin and conditioned through faulty thinking, otherwise these less fortunate individuals would suffer continually and that is not so.

Superconscious Activity

Few of us seem to appreciate that we constantly

utilize our five normal physical senses throughout our daily lives without experiencing any undue fatigue (unless any one is subjected to excessive abuse, when Nature usually intervenes in its own particular way). There should therefore be even less cause for any form of physical tiredness other than that brought about by walking, as the mental forces exercised in dowsing are dependent on superconscious activity which requires little or no conscious effort; and once some experience has been gained, the process becomes almost automatic.

There are in fact endless ways in which a relationship between the conscious side of our make-up and its counterpart, the subconscious, can be established, and many of the devious methods of approach are in reality manifestations of this indirect principle. Some dowsers are only able to work through the use of serial numbers. This is a very individualistic approach in which the mind is pre-conditioned to associate a particular number with a 'pre-allocated object likely to be encountered, and the numbers naturally vary with different dowsers. But why complicate matters when the *direct* thought of the object is available, since the use of such a system is dependent on an unnecessary conditioning process likely to encourage error?

Samples

I have so far tried to provide a broad outline of the various forces responsible for the dowsing manifestation, and the different approaches adopted by dowsers. In the next section I will attempt to describe some of the elaborate instruments that have been devised to assist man in this field. In addition, many supplementary aids, like the serial numbers method, are used.

The most popular of these is the sample, so this deserves special attention.

The use of samples can certainly be justified in the earlier stages of developing the art as they can greatly aid concentration, but such a practice should be discouraged once familiarity has been established with all matter likely to be encountered. At first, I believed a sample was necessary because I had unknowingly been conditioned to think so, but on trying out a few experiments, I soon realized that, as in the case of Mager's Rosette, it didn't make any difference what sample was being held in my mind (and I had made up a selection of ten small opaque phials containing different matter), for my rods would only react to what I had *mentally* visualized.

Naturally, there are very good reasons for using samples in the location of missing people or lost objects, and particularly unfamiliar material, for every possible sense we possess must be employed in communication with the superconscious, and that includes the physical, to compensate for the lack of information normally derived from other sources, but it must be the right kind of sample the selection of which can be very difficult at times. There is always a tendency for a rational, subconscious wishful thought to intervene in the process which, on crystallization, gets amplified through auto-suggestion, thus resulting in a false interpretation in spite of sincere intentions. In addition, the use of samples can mislead our findings, for the pre-conditioned mental picture of what we are seeking and the characteristics of the object being held (which is invariably placed in a phial made from an entirely different substance) don't always entirely coincide.

Aerial Dowsing

It would be difficult to find a more suitable
explanation for aerial dowsing than the use of the
superconscious. When I was first approached by
an American concern engaged in the mining of
ores in the Middle East, I had some doubts as to
my ability in view of the large areas involved and
how difficult it might be to pinpoint the regions
of mineral activity. I explained to them that it
should, in principle, be possible to dowse from
an aeroplane but as I had no experience of this, it
would be better if I were first subjected to some
tests. They agreed but wished to carry them out
under realistic conditions, so I was flown out
there on a 'no result – no fee' basis.

When it had been ascertained that there was
no obvious geographical means whereby
physical appearances could be associated with
rock bearing ore, I was asked to dowse over a
number of mountainous regions which, though
I did not know it, included eight preselected
active spots. On my return I was greeted with a
jovial, 'O.K., fella, we're in business.' I had got
seven out of the eight right and the Americans
gave me VIP treatment throughout my visit,
which was rather enjoyable.

Although not entirely relevant to our subject,
there are endless ways in which the
superconscious can be used to personal
advantage once its development has been
thoroughly established and an awareness of its
potential realized. For example, it can be
demonstrated in a very spectacular and
convincing manner by an experienced
practitioner – with a willing witness – who can
drive a reasonably fast car on the wrong side of
a narrow road will a number of blind bends in
the knowledge that there will be *no* oncoming

vehicles, and such an ability when applied to congested traffic conditions can greatly reduce wasted time.

Obviously, such experiments must never be conducted by any but the most competent of practitioners, but there are nevertheless many less dangerous ways of encouraging this faculty whilst on the road. One is to constantly try to 'feel' the next approaching car and determine in advance its type and colour. After some practice, it is surprising to find how accurate you can become, indicating that forces other than chance are at work. With a little more experience, even part of the registration numbers can be 'guessed' in advance – some children seem to be very good at this game.

CHAPTER FOUR

DOWSING INSTRUMENTS

There are many different instruments, or amplifiers as I prefer to call them, but the majority of them have one characteristic in common. They nearly all rely on the production of a state of balanced instability whereupon the slightest change in movement tends to break down the equilibrium. The more simple devices, such as pendulums, or L-shaped rods, depend solely on the combined twisting action of the forearms or wrists. Both of these types are functionally the same although they do have their relative merits.

'L'Rods

The 'L' rods, which are directly dependent on the amplification of minute muscular movements tending to twist the arms, are the simplest and probably the easiest tool for locating straightforward subterranean matter such as streams or pipe-lines. Newcomers to the art will invariably find that the 'L' rods function, though neither the forked twig nor the pendulum are effective.

This device should be made from metal rods of at least a quarter of an inch in diameter to ensure that they are not too easily swayed by cross winds, and shaped as indicated.

18 inches

5 inches

(Dimensions to be adjusted to suit individual requirements.)

The construction is in fact unimportant, but if it is believed to be influential, an alloy such as welding rod can be used as this would eliminate the hypothetical question of attraction or repellence.

The rods are loosely held one in each hand with the small finger on the inside to ensure they remain parallel to the ground whilst projecting forwards. On passing over the selected object, they will either turn inwards or outwards depending on our pre-conditioned approach.

The Pendulum

The pendulum, apart from its physical sensitivity to air movement, gives similar results, but its operator must be quite sure that the relationship of outer physical movements to inner mental activity is properly co-ordinated for, unlike the angle rods, the varying reactions can easily be entirely misinterpreted. Personally, I have always conditioned my mind to associate clockwise gyrations with positive responses and the reverse with negative ones, whilst plain oscillations represent indifference or a neutral attitude. Once I have tuned in to the particular object I am looking for, I set the pendulum oscillating and on reaching the object the original swinging movements are instantly converted to clockwise gyrations. But the choice is a personal one and some dowsers prefer to begin their approach to such an application with the pendulum motionless.

Because the pendulum lends itself to the subconscious self-questioning process from which all kinds of information can be gathered, it is used for food and beverage analysis, medical diagnosis and treatment, map dowsing, and the locating of objects, and if one also happens to be gifted with additional ESP faculties, there are no limits to the benefits one can bestow on humanity.

Both these instruments can be used in determining direction. With the rods, it is merely a matter of standing in an area where, for example, it is thought that there may be an underground stream, and slowly turning on one's axis holding out the rods in the projected position. When facing the nearest accumulation of water, the rods will begin to react accordingly. The same procedure is followed with the pendulum but here the free arm can be extended to pinpoint the direction just that bit more accurately.

To many, the location of a missing object is as much as they want to achieve, but in the more complicated versions of dowsing work has barely begun at this point. Water is a good example, for additional information such as depth and potential yield are essential before any authority

can justify excavations. Because of the many
personal methods of approach employed in
determining these details, a degree of
unreliability does seem to exist and this tends to
undermine the reputation of the more competent
dowser.

The Triangular Method

Many techniques are employed to locate and
obtain the more elusive information about a
stream, but the triangular method is quite a
reliable example. When the width of a stream
has been determined by approaching it from
both sides at right angles and marking its
boundaries with pegs, one walks away from it, at
the same time increasing concentration and
sensitivity in order to pick up another but weaker
signal to the stream. When the signal is located
and its distance measured from the centre of the
stream, this distance invariably corresponds to
its depth.

Still further away, an even weaker signal can
be detected, and the distance separating this one
from the depth parallel can be interpreted to
indicate actual flow by stepping it out,
multiplying the number of paces by ten and
calling the result gallons per hour. Here a little
additional local knowledge or experience can be
useful, since the structure of the soil through
which these supposed radiations pass can
influence them in some way. This is particularly
noticeable when clay is encountered, so must be
taken into account when preparing one's final
figures.

Great caution must always be exercised by
hyper-sensitive dowsers employing this method,
however, particularly in spacious unfamiliar
areas, as difficulty can so easily be experienced in

differentiating and isolating the various signals received, resulting in an unreliable interpretation of the actual existing conditions. A couple of such conclusions with influential concerns will put an end to that dowsing career.

The same procedure can be followed when using the pendulum, but this is not really necessary as merely by standing on top of the stream and adopting the self-questioning process already referred to, all the other operations can be eliminated, indicating that in reality we are aware of the rods' limitations. To compensate for this and ensure reliable results, some additional work becomes necessary.

Direction of Flow

With regard to determining direction of flow, immediate surroundings must not be permitted to influence judgement, for subterranean strata frequently bear no relationship to surface formation, and an aquifer (a formation containing sufficient water to supply wells, etc.) may well flow in the opposite direction to a surface incline. All that is necessary is to walk in a line over the stream, believing firmly that the rods or pendulum will react when walking against the flow, and that is precisely what they will do.

To elaborate on the unexpected behaviour of aquifers, many unusual experiences have been known, but I include here just one personal example associated with my well in the grounds of my home which, at a height of almost 800 feet, is the highest in Sussex. Being a hydrologist and rather methodically inclined, I liked to keep a record of the relationship of rainfall to the water table. Consequently, daily readings were taken from a float-operated graduated dial installed beneath the well-head and, when applicable, these were related to the rain gauge. Naturally, there would always be a slight delay in the rise of the well's water level in relation to sudden rainfall, but during the dry summer of 1959, when it had not rained for at least six weeks, the level rose by just over six feet in two days.

My first reaction was to conclude that a cracked water main was responsible for the sudden rise, but on checking both the boundaries of the stream feeding the well and all possible deviations within the area with my rods, I could find no unusual activity so I decided to extract a sample for analysis and take the findings to the Geological Museum in London.

I was astounded to learn that in some parts of south-east England, wells occasionally penetrated aquifers containing water originating from hundreds of miles away, due to flows being reversed under special conditions – but some more information on these hydrological matters will be given later. In my case, the sample was typical of water found in certain regions of the Continent. I formed my own conclusions accordingly, bearing in mind that the water found in many oases today may have fallen on the Earth's surface 2000 years ago and advanced to that particular area at a rate of only a few inches per day. It is equally strange that my particular well, with a depth of thirty feet and at that relative height, should never have run dry when 400 yards *down* the road, a ninety-foot well in the grounds of our council offices is invariably dry and useless.

More Instruments

To revert to instruments, however, reference has already been made to the 'Revealer' invented by

L.J. Veale, and this, compared with some of the more sophisticated devices I saw being used by so-called dowsers in the Caribbean and the States, is relatively cheap. One of my clients had purchased the 'Universal Antenna Rod', with its beautifully finished, heavy, chromium-plated parts and built-in 'magnetic tubes'. Although it was basically only a pair of L-shaped rods fitted with unnecessary refinements, it cost a small fortune (290 dollars at the time of my visit in 1974) and it was claimed by both the manufacturer and my client that it could 'automatically' point to and locate any required mineral, including gold and silver, within a twenty-mile radius and to a depth of fifty feet. I was so astounded by these claims that I managed to persuade its owner to let me keep the relevant brochure and it makes fantastic reading to this day. But his faith in this magnificent 'detector' must have been weaker than supposed in view of his request for my services.

I also met the owner of a 'Spanish Dip Needle', complete with its 'mineral load capable of multiplying the body's electrostatic energy several times over', which could be used on its own as a pendulum or be screwed into an adaptor fitted on top of the supplied pair of forked divining rods. Here too, however, the results had been very disappointing. In these and several other cases I encountered, a basic sensitivity on the part of the operators was lacking, and it is extremely unfair of manufactueres of such equipment to guarantee results knowing the gullibility of the public and the personal diversity of the dowsing process. On principle, I tried both these instruments and several others incorporating springs and various gadgets, but none surpassed the effectiveness of my cheap old L-shaped welding rods and simple plastic pendulum.

There is of course no limit to the number of devices that can be designed and shaped to provide a means whereby the slightest change in muscular control can be amplified, but the 'Motorscope', which consists only of a piece of wire shaped like a crank with an indicating pointer positioned on its central portion, is a good example of a really effective, simple and inexpensive device. In fact, just such an instrument was used by many well-established dowsers of the past, including Major C.A. Pogson, M.C., who was at one time the official dowser to the Bombay Government, and Miss Evelyn Penrose who worked for the Government of British Columbia.

Reactions of the Operator

In a way, there can be no simpler instrument than the pendulum but, as with all devices, it is the way the operator has programmed his mental process that determines the reactions obtained and the effectiveness of its use. If one really believes that the length of the thread supporting a pendulum is capable of determining the 'harmonic frequency' of an object being sought, or if one attaches a particular significance to gyrations as opposed to oscillations as a result of having been subconsciously conditioned by others to think that way, then the mind will be programmed to respond to just those instructions.

Before time can be influential in preventing the rejection of certain ideas, however, it is well worth while to reflect and analyse one's own particular tendencies and re-programme one's mind to the acceptance of a more rational approach. In other words, think for yourself in terms of your own abilities and don't allow the experience of others to cloud your judgement, thereby adding confusion to the 'computer'.

To go to extremes, there are many dowsers who genuinely believe their instruments will not function in the dark or under moonlight conditions, whilst others are quite convinced that if one of their sleeves happens to be rolled up, this too will prevent the rods from working. Again, there are those who firmly believe that pendulums hollowed out to hold samples will only operate when held in the left hand or that they will only gyrate clockwise over all minerals and metals which are good conductors of electricity and counter-clockwise over other objects.

In effect, it's all in the mind. But one last word about the self-questioning process with regard to the determination of depth with a pendulum. All that has to be done here is to stand over the stream, having set the pendulum oscillating, and mentally count in appropriate depth units with complete confidence that, on reaching the required depth, gyrations will follow. This principle is equally applicable to rods.

CHAPTER FIVE

HYDROLOGICAL ASPECTS OF DOWSING

Dowsing has been practised for centuries for all kinds of matter, but in the majority of cases water has been the objective. Though not wishing to seem presumptuous, I as a water engineer have found on several occasions that people practising or interested in dowsing have had a very limited idea about the behaviour of subterranean water, and it is because of this lack of knowledge that a few non-technical references are included in the hope that they may throw light on disappointing results.

To begin with, reference must be made to the basic hydrological cycle which repeats itself indefinitely, although in certain areas the process can sometimes be prolonged over many years, thereby causing a great deal of hardship to humanity. In principle, it states briefly that the sun's heat rays evaporate large quantities of the ocean's waters, and this moist or saturated warm air is carried away by trade winds over cooler land regions where it condenses into clouds and is finally discharged back on to the earth's surface as rain. It then begins to make its way back to the sea.

However, not all this surface water returns to the sea – between thirty and fifty per cent of it percolates underground and it is this portion which seems so much more interesting, for its behaviour is not so obvious.

This country has such consistent rainfall that it is considered to be very well supplied with water, but in reality an ever-increasing demand is forcing our engineers towards the extraction of water from underground sources.

Unlike surface water, flows or movements beneath the ground are very slow indeed, rarely exceeding a few feet per day in normal strata, for they are entirely dependent on the gradients, temperature and hydraulic properties of the soil through which they pass.[1]

In certain parts of the world, such as the

[1] For the technically inclined, the rate of movement for underground water depends on hydrostatic pressures and soil permeability, but the principal factors are gravity and

Libyan Desert, it very rarely rains and, as previously explained, small communities live in oases where they are entirely dependent on the extraction of water from aquifers replenished from rainful that landed on a distant region many years ago. Provided the extraction rate is within the natural supply limits, the community continues to thrive and this is why their population invariably remains static.

Temperatures and Underground Flow

It may also seem surprising to some that temperature can have an important bearing on underground 'flow', particularly in this country where extremes of ambient temperature are not great, but an increase or decrease of ten degrees from the accepted average of forty-nine degrees Fahrenheit will alter a 'flow' by seventeen per cent and such a difference could be of great importance to yield under certain circumstances.

There are cases where unexpected holes on the surface of the earth take in water and discharge it elsewhere, such as the water that disappears into the Malham Tarn in Yorkshire and comes up again in Malham Cove, where the River Aire originates as a 'spring'. Sometimes, there are definite subterranean water courses which are followed by rivers in times of drought.

It is very difficult to ascertain the rate of

---

molecular attraction of surface tension. If soil pores are large, the flows will tend to follow basic hydraulic laws, but if they are small, molecular attraction will play an important part. The porosity is the percentage of voids in the soil, based on the total volume of the mass including the voids. The effective size of the soil is the size of the grain that is larger than ten per cent by weight of the particles composing the soil.

movement of underground water accurately,
and it can only be found by the arduous process
of sinking numerous small wells into aquifers
and following introduced dyes, or by using the
services of a competent dowser which should be
far more economical. The results were very
satisfying when I compared the two approaches
over a calculated period in my garden, where a
few deep holes remain to this day.

Three Zones

Underground water is found in three zones,
which for convenience could be termed the
Upper, Middle and Lower Zones. The Upper
Zone, which is just below the surface of the
ground, contains water that has risen from the
Middle Zone through capillary action and is
held in place by the soil pore spaces. The Middle
Zone consists of a mixture of air and water
suspended in the soil pore spaces. The Lower
Zone is the saturated area, the top of which is
termed the water table and, as was seen from the
reference to my well, this has little bearing on the
surrounding contour of the ground's surface.

The extraction of water from aquifers is
carried out by means of pumping machinery
suitably placed in or adjacent to wells,
depending on their depth. The exception is the
Artesian well, which is positioned on an aquifer
that has passed through one or more impervious
strata and penetrated an area containing water
under pressure, thereby enabling it to rise on its
own.

There is also the 'flowing well', where the top
is lower than some of the raised portions of the
pervious strata in the area, and this will act as a
spring under heavy rainfall; but these are not
often seen as they are usually indicative of faulty

location. Springs occur as a result of rain falling on pervious rocks that have become saturated. The excess is discharged at the nearest exposed area above an impervious stratum. The actual conditions under which this can happen vary a good deal but the principle is always the same.

It is also possible to locate large quantities of water in catchment areas where the impervious rocks have been formed into a natural bowl from which the water cannot escape, because the limited rainfall does not permit the water table to rise to a sufficiently high level to enable the excess to 'overflow' as either a spring or subterranean stream. The rate of evaporation by capillary action through the Upper Zone or pervious stratum has become equal to the rainfall, with the result that water extracted from such static areas is frequently quite unsuitable for domestic use.

Seeking Flowing Water

Bearing this in mind, the reliable dowser must always seek water from areas where genuine underground circulation exists and preferably from that which has risen through fissures, many of which originate from subterranean streams – Nature's underground safety valves – and not from descending waters. The latter may have passed through insufficient pervious strata to effect satisfactory filtration and also, depending on the depth, may have been contaminated from surface activity, thereby rendering them useless.

It is not my intention to relate the history of wells, for they no doubt began as mere excavations in the sides of rocks and hills where water could be found flowing near the surface. In all probability, it was one of these shallow streams that Moses smote with his rod – or could that part of the biblical text have been mistranslated and the true meaning be that Moses was in fact a dowser?

Difficulty is frequently experienced in selecting the most favourable location to sink a well and if the physical conditions are such that it is obviously necessary to bore to a great depth, the situation usually resolves itself into one requiring geological knowledge and sound judgement. But, in spite of considerable scepticism, many engineers and geologists are becoming more lenient towards the engagement of a competent dowser who has made a scientific study of the art and has a sound engineering training.

Dowsing and Geology

I have on occasions worked with geologists who have determined, from their knowledge of the stratification and general physical features of an area, the existence of water at a certain depth, but, on boring, have been proved to be incorrect. Normally, geologists are correct in their findings but their superior knowledge does not help when having to determine the exact location for a well over water-bearing strata that is fissured, for an error of only a few feet may result in complete failure. A dowser, however, can sense such a fault immediately.

Some time ago, I was approached by a firm of consultants who had already employed the services of geologists with disappointing results, and had decided as a last resort to give dowsing the opportunity to prove itself. It was necessary to locate a small supply of water on the top of a hill for the cooling of electronic equipment of a proposed Satellite Tracking Station abroad. The geologists evidently maintained there was none available, but they had based their findings on strata knowledge rather than the human ability to locate fresh aquifers trapped between impervious layers of rock. On surveying the area very carefully, I finally located a small underground stream, which was tapped accordingly and provided a yield of approximately 300 gallons per hour. This proved to be sufficient for their needs and, taking into account the fact that the survey was carried out during the summer, there was every reason to suppose the yield would increase during the winter months, as later proved to be the case.

On the whole, dowsers of the past have not created a very favourable impression in professional circles, and though the question of water divining is often raised when water supply is discussed, most water engineers deny its existence. Its reputation has suffered as much from its friends as from its enemies, the over-statements of the former having provided ample ammunition for the latter, and this situation is not likely to improve whilst there is no governing body controlling the interests of the would-be dowser.

CHAPTER SIX

FINER ASPECTS OF THE DOWSING PHENOMENON

The merits of the more subtle and intangible forces involved in the dowsing phenomenon, such as radiesthesia, map dowsing and many of the other inexplicable manifestations related to this latent power in humanity, are increasingly difficult to discuss as all the varying methods of approach involved are actuated through very personal self-conditioned processes which, in spite of the very remarkable results obtained, can be both direct and very indirect.

As a dowser, I always expressed keen interest in all these other fields of activity, and in fact employed map dowsing on a number of occasions as an alternative to long and not always justified journeys. My work with radiesthesia was invariably limited to the instant removal of headaches or minor ailments from both the family and personal friends, but neither of these activities ever equalled my enthusiasm for practical dowsing until I was unexpectedly called upon by a gentleman who happened to be a practising radiesthesist.

Evidently, Mr Donald Munro, a long-standing member of the BSD, had read one of my articles in the Society's journal and when by chance he was passing near to my home, he thought it might be a good idea to call and make my acquaintance. In no time, we were involved in a deep discussion beginning with dowsing in general and ending with radiesthesia in particular. He claimed he could pass his hands over the contour of a fully-clothed person without actually making physical contact, and instantly feel if there was anything wrong either internally or externally.

Such a claim proved to be too much of a temptation and I suggested he might like to have a go with me. I wasn't very impressed when, beginning with my hands, he informed me that I might be experiencing some tightness in the forearms due to muscular tension. On reaching my left shoulder, however, his hand was suddenly repelled by some violent inexplicable force and he immediately exclaimed that I had had some kind of accident at one time and that

the bones had not knitted together quite as
Nature would have wished. I was astounded. He
was quite right, for many years ago I had
smashed my shoulder in a motorbike accident in
France.

Dependence on Electrical Aids

It was therefore not surprising that I
immediately began to develop a far keener
interest in this field. I was invited to a Society
specializing in this activity, where I found that
the majority of its equally enthusiastic members
believed in the necessity for some rather
extraordinary electrical 'aids' which included
the 'Black Box', but my analytical mind just
could not accept their explanations for the
phenomenon, particularly since Mr Munro's
remarkable success had not been dependent on
instrumentation of any kind.

Naturally, I couldn't deny the results they had
obtained but felt these aids were unnecessary
and, having been a Charge Engineer in power
stations, the temptation to dismantle one of the
more advanced 'Black Boxes' became
irresistible. I was absolutely amazed to find that
the contents were simple circuits and that, in
addition, many of the elaborate dials were not
even connected to circuits of any kind, indicating
that these highly expensive machines were really
only acting as focusing aids to the mind.

On suggesting this to one of the manufacturers
of these machines, however, I was informed that,
should the 'settings' inadvertently be misplaced,
very serious repercussions might follow. Here
again, the challenge was too great, and naturally
I suffered no ill effects, but when we consider the
hold Dr Abrams' diagnostic device (originally
called the ERA, standing for the Electric

Reactor of Dr Abrams) has had and is still having both in America and other countries, this is in itself quite an achievement.

In fact, a thorough investigation was finally carried out by a team of experts consisting of radio engineers, doctors, civil engineers, and a telepathic spiritualist just in case thought waves were involved, and the results were reported in the magazine *Scientific American*. It was discovered that the 'occillocast', as it was sometimes called, was only a condenser, a rheostat, an ohmmeter and a magnetic interrupter, the combination of which could never be instrumental in influencing anyone. At best, the investigators concluded, 'It is all an illusion, at worst, it is a colossal fraud.'

In Radiesthesia, as with all branches of the subject, practitioners precondition themselves into certain approaches, one of which is that clockwise gyrations represent healthy conditions and the reverse some form of sickness, the severity of which is determined either by the distance of the hand from the body, or the number of oscillations.

General Rules

Depending on one's attitude of mind and the application involved, the basic ingredients of map dowsing are that the pendulum is held in one hand, a suitable indicator to pinpoint a particular area in the other, and that a map with as large a scale as is practicable is used to encourage accuracy.

As a general rule, I am not in favour of samples but there are exceptions, and if one is entirely unfamiliar with the object being sought or, as is sometimes the case, the person being located, a really reliable sample can be invaluable as the process is one requiring quite a high degree of concentration and such an addition will tend to counteract any distractions likely to be encountered.

When using samples, it is vital that they represent precisely what is being sought. In the case of inanimate objects, this rarely presents a problem, but when dealing with people, the only really dependable items are hair or blood, although clothing and close belongings such as personal letters can be almost as effective.

If there is no clue at all as to the whereabouts of whatever is being sought, it is necessary either to employ the self-questioning process with a pendulum or to use maps of different sizes, gradually decreasing the scale until one is reached from which no difficulty is experienced in extracting the required information. Here, mention must be made of the fact that many dowsers believe it is essential, before operations can begin, for the maps to be placed in the correct direction. In other words, the indicated north on the map must point to magnetic north, hence the need for compasses in certain cases, though with a little practice, this can be determined without one.

This additional use of the dowsing faculty to determine orientation and direction can be employed very effectively at times, particularly in a country where the sun is frequently obscured by cloud. But even then, things can go wrong if the method is not used selectively.

I always remember the one occasion I attempted to make use of it to take a short cut home. When I came to a major crossroads without a signpost, I got out of the car armed with my angle rods and immediately ascertained that I should turn left rather than go straight on. But I had inadvertently asked the wrong question, so determining the correct *direction* of my home in relation to my position but not the most practical way of getting there. I followed the selected road for a while and though it later began to twist and turn, I hoped that the direction would correct itself. In the end, however, I was obliged to return to the crossroads and start again, arriving home far later than expected. It is therefore essential, when attempting to obtain information of this kind, that the approach is backed by the combination of both intelligence and a very clear mental picture of the envisaged requirements.

CHAPTER SEVEN

A SUMMARY

As personal progress is made in the exploration of this extremely wide and interesting subject, it will be found that there are countless approaches and deviations from accepted general principles. Some of these seem highly irrational or even downright stupid, and so have not been included here, but it is known that many do produce reliable results, indicating that, regardless of its origin, the force responsible for these activities is largely indifferent to our personal attitudes – within reason.

As previously explained, there are those who dowse in a quiet, inoffensive way but experience extreme tiredness due to its supposed weakening effects, whilst others literally have wild and violent contortions, completely opposing those able to dowse without any form of instrumentation. As a result of these extreme variations, the art has become associated with unconventional beings possessing peculiar ideas, but though this ability makes us a little different, we are not abnormal.

To those of suitable temperament, being a dowser can become quite an asset in social circles, as most 'curiosities' invariably become the centre of attraction. Alternatively, this knowledge can become a hindrance to freedom if one is being constantly approached and asked to provide demonstrations or give lectures.

Testing the Ability

I have met many intellectual people with a sceptical side to their nature who, on hearing of my ability, immediately wanted to subject my powers to elaborate tests. But apart from those carried out by Professor John Cohen at Manchester University in the interests of science, I rarely get involved in tests for I believe all Nature's gifts should be utilized for their proper purpose. If it is a case of foreseeing an application and someone needs to be reassured or satisfied that such an ability is a reality, on the other hand, that is quite a different matter.

On just such an occasion, I had been staying with a couple of friends of mine in their apartment in New York and, the day before my departure for home, I was reluctantly asked whether I would very much mind being subjected to a dowsing test in the interests of future applications. Naturally, I conceded to his request and we went down to a sidewalk adjacent to his building in East 52nd Street, armed with my rods, a tape measure, pencil and paper, and a piece of chalk.

Needless to say, neither of us had any idea what lay beneath the sidewalk, but after a short while, whilst my friend recorded my findings both on paper and on the wall, I located all the services individually, making particular reference to the water main as it incorporated an acute bend right in the middle of the sidewalk. I also located a small tunnel which I felt sure was a sewer.

Eventually, because the superintendent of the block was not familiar with the position of all the services, my friend was obliged to contact the original architects and I finally received written confirmation that all my findings had been one hundred per cent correct, including the bent water main.

As I have said, it is strange how we, as supposedly advanced creatures, should be so backward in the development of our self-protective instincts in relation to some of the simpler forms of animal life, and I am not referring specifically to dowsing but to the other potential ESP faculties which could still be encouraged through the adoption of a more natural way of life.

I have only described experiments which tend to support the generally accepted views on dowsing, and have not devoted a separate section to experiments that might be tried at home. The reason for this is that such suggestions pre-condition a reader to think in a particular way, and a collection of experiments covering this wide field would only lead to inner confusion. By all means try experiments, but let them be ones originating in your own mind, for they will then automatically be acceptable to your own particular self-suggestive process. In fact, once the idea has been conceived, put into effect and worked satisfactorily, you will have become a dowser.